A Grocer, Soldier and His Horse

Adapted from a Satsang story by Sant Ram Singh Ji on August 5, 2016

Illustrated by Carlos Brito

GO JOLLY
BOOKS

A Grocer, Soldier and His Horse

A Grocer, Soldier and His Horse is a story originally told in Satsang by Sant Ram Singh Ji on August 5, 2016 during a Meditation Retreat Program at RadhaSwami Ashram, Channasandra Village, Karnataka, India.

Translated by Ashok Shinkar
Transcribed by Ali Czernin, Geoff Halstead, & Harvey Rosenberg

Many thanks to those who reviewed & critiqued the story:
some sevadars

Special thanks to our Illustrator:
Carlos stated that the more he illustrates our stories, the more he likes them. Well, he must really have liked this story because his illustrations in this book are beyond outstanding. They magically are bursting with beauty and joy, and a touch of humor. We're blessed to have Carlos illustrate our books. Thank you, dear Carlos.

ISBN: 978-1-942937-24-1

(c) 2017 All Rights Reserved

Published by
Go Jolly Books
www.gojollybooks.com
P.O. Box 2203, Port Angeles, WA 98362 USA

A Grocer, Soldier and His Horse

Adapted from a Satsang story by Sant Ram Singh Ji on August 5, 2016

INTRODUCTION

A Grocer, Soldier and His Horse is a true story that Sawan Singh Ji Maharaj often told in Satsang. It shows that whatever we do in this lifetime will undoubtedly affect our lives to come. In other words, "what we sow, we reap," whether we're conscious of our actions or not. We cannot escape our fate karma.

A Grocer, Soldier and His Horse is a simple story with great importance. We cannot blame our present-day circumstances on our Master, on our family, friends, or enemies. We are living our lives based on what we have done in the past, i.e., what we ourselves have done, so who is there to blame?

In January, 2014, at RadhaSwami Ashram, Channasandra Village, Karnataka, India, Sant Ram Singh Ji gave me permission to take stories He told in Satsang and publish them as books for children. He has allowed me to change His words directed to adults to words suitable for children. With His Limitless Grace, reviewers of the first twelve books have told us children like the books.

Once again, Carlos Brito has given us joyous illustrations to accompany the words. His imaginative use of color coupled with his creative skills make whimsical characters and beautiful scenery.

A Grocer, Soldier and His Horse will hopefully further sink into children's and adult's hearts the importance of following the Teaching of our Masters. We hope you enjoy it.

Radhaswami,
Harvey Rosenberg

Dedication

Only with Sant Ram Singh Ji's Limitless Grace has this book come to us. We are more appreciative and grateful than our words can ever express.

Here's a Ram Singh quotation from January 4, 2017 Meditation Talk:

"So, it is always the Grace of the Masters,
Who get seva done by the disciples, and then,
let them get the praise for doing that seva also."

That's our situation with the books.

Sawan Singh Ji Maharaj traveled from camp to camp while in the military. In each camp, vendors would sell groceries and other supplies to the army personnel. In one particular camp, Sawan Singh and others, including a young soldier who had no family, regularly purchased what they needed from the same grocer.

The soldiers received cash salaries, which they would deposit with one of the grocers, because, in those days, there were very few banks to maintain accounts. Soldiers would then buy supplies from that grocer.

At this time, India and Afghanistan were colonies of the British Empire. When war broke out between Afghanistan and the British, many Indians went to fight on behalf of the British government.

The young soldier who had no family was one of the men who fought in the war. Every day, he rode his horse into battle and returned. One day his mare panicked and mistakenly ran into enemy territory. Engulfed by the enemy, both the horse and soldier were killed.

At the time of his death, the soldier was thinking, "I should not have died like this. It's my horse's fault. Had she not run behind enemy lines, I wouldn't have died."

He also remembered that the grocer had a lot of his money. He thought, "That money is going to be wasted. I have no family to inherit it."

In this way, he died thinking that his horse caused his death and the grocer had all his money.

A few years later, the grocer's contract with the army expired and the grocer put the shop up for sale. He sold it to the highest bidder, collected his belongings, and returned to live in his home city of Jalandhar. There, he built a house and got married.

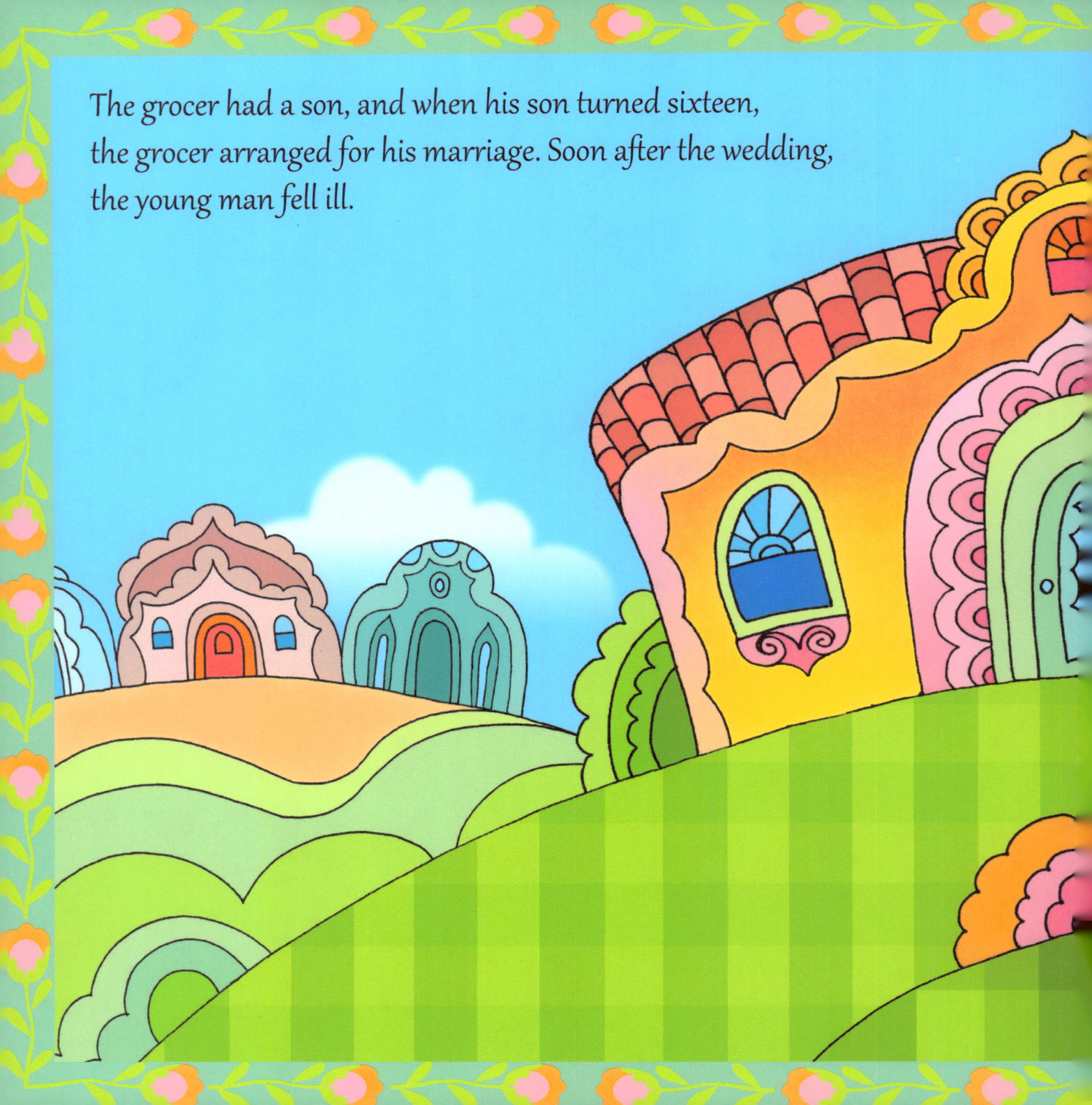

The grocer had a son, and when his son turned sixteen, the grocer arranged for his marriage. Soon after the wedding, the young man fell ill.

Over a month, he was bedridden and despite the help of various doctors, his health deteriorated. As he was dying, he became aware of events that had happened in his previous life.

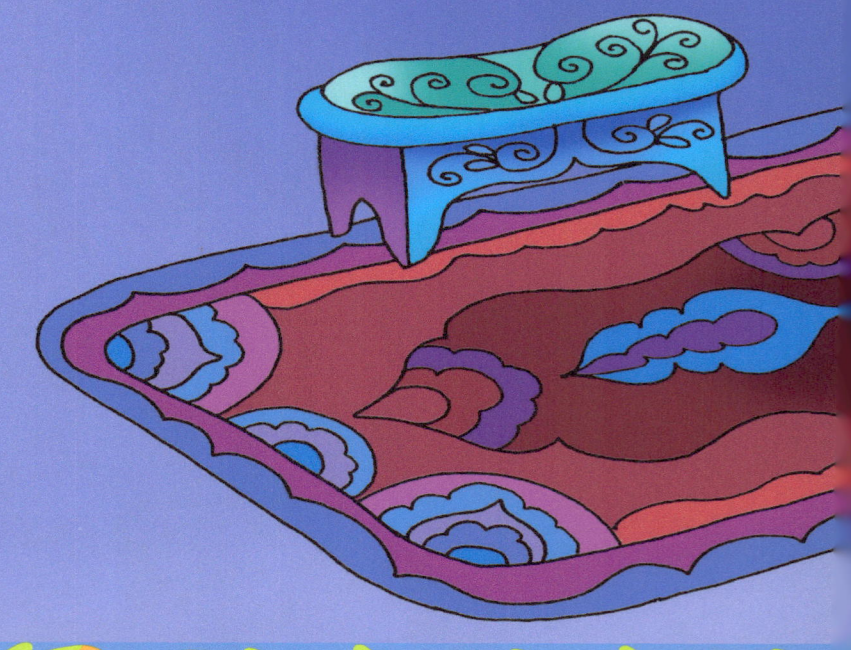

His father was sitting by his bedside crying. The son said to him, "Don't cry. Don't cry for me.

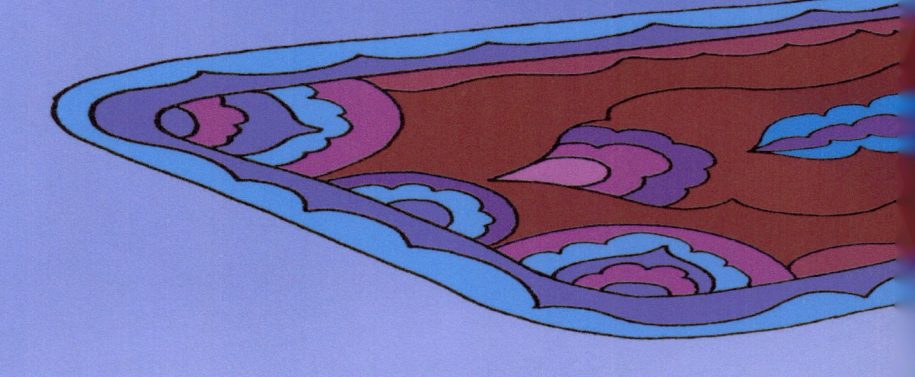

I am the soldier who shopped in your store and to whom you owed money. You have fed me, educated me, and cared for me all these years with that money. Now, our account is clear."

"My wife was the horse who took me to my death. I suffered a lot while dying. Now, she will suffer for the rest of her life, because we have only been married a short time and she will now be a widow."
(In India at that time, women did not remarry when their husbands died.)

About two years after the young man died, Baba Sawan Singh Ji, now retired, went to Jalandhar and happened to meet this same grocer. They had been friends during their time in the army.
The grocer saluted Sawan Singh and invited Him to his house.

Sawan Singh Ji Maharaj accepted the grocer's invitation, went to his house, and was offered something to eat.

While there, Sawan Singh heard someone crying. Although a few years had passed since the grocer's son had died, his widow still broke down in tears when people visited.

Sawan Singh Ji Maharaj heard her crying and said to the grocer, "Look, why are you serving me? When there is some sorrow in your house, I don't feel that you should be serving me."

The grocer told Him, "Maharaj, this is the world. So, don't worry. Please eat."

But Sawan Singh Ji Maharaj insisted, and said, "Definitely, there is sadness in your house. Until you tell me what's going on, I'm unable to accept your food."

So then, the grocer related the whole story about the camp, the soldier and his horse, and how he had died.

He said, "This is what has happened. The soldier has died and the horse is crying. So, why should I consider that a sorrow? They're completing their fate karma, and there's nothing that can be done. Why should I be sad?"

Other Books Adapted From Satsangs Given By Sant Ram Singh Ji

www.ingramcontent.com/pod-product-compliance
Lightning Source LLC
Chambersburg PA
CBHW041227040426
42444CB00002B/81